CARTOLINA
DALLA
CUCINA

Bruno Barbieri

Do you tagine?

Photography by **Riccardo Lettieri**

BIBLIOTHECA CULINARIA

The tagine... a new way of cooking

In Western kitchens the term "tagine" retains an aura of the exotic but, in reality, behind this word of Berber origin lies a cooking technique with which you are probably already familiar, one that may be employed with conventional ingredients. Like the wok, another decidedly non-Western utensil, the tagine simply takes a little getting used to in order to appreciate its versatility. With time and practice it will no longer seem like an unusual utensil in the kitchen, and you will find that it can be used in many different ways. A symbol of the special conviviality that comes with one-dish meals, the tagine is also an attractive object. It seems a pity to relegate it to the top shelf of the cupboard when its rightful place is in the centre of a warm welcoming kitchen.

Before you can make the tagine truly your own, a few basic facts are in order. The term "tagine" refers to both the cooking vessel itself and the food that is prepared in it. The vessel consists of two parts: a round base that can be used both for cooking and serving and a cone-shaped cover or lid whose form facilitates the circulation of condensed cooking vapour back to the bottom of the tagine and into the food. The steam trapped inside slowly infuses the food with flavour while cooking it at the same time. Today, tagines are available in a range of different materials, but glazed clay remains the most popular choice as well as the most practical one. The term "tagine", when used to refer to a dish, does not have a precise identity and is often characterized by its principal ingredient: lamb tagine, prawn tagine, etc.

Traditional use of the tagine is based on a long slow cooking process at a low temperature. One school of thought holds that once all of the ingredients have been placed in the base, they should be left undisturbed until they are completely cooked. Recipes based on North African dishes tend to adopt this system, partly because of local tradition (formerly tagines were placed on burning coals to cook) and partly because of the ingredients used (more economical cuts of meat). This slow cooking method, using the steam produced inside the container to cook the food, is very similar to the western method of braising. In reality, the tagine can be used to perfection for any type of traditional braised dishes. When time is not an issue, this method of long slow cooking at low temperatures provides excellent results, but the interesting feature of tagine cooking is that it is not limited to these conditions.

The recipes that follow demonstrate the versatility of the tagine. By using combinations of cooking techniques, employing more or less of the enclosed steam and by varying the sequence in which single ingredients are placed in the tagine, it is possible to obtain food consistencies which are very different from those associated with traditional braised dishes. The deep base of the tagine can also accommodate a fair amount of liquid, making it a perfect choice for preparing dishes more akin to traditional casseroles. Finally, with its elegant form, updated colour selection and easy passage from oven to table, today's tagine is worthy of its place in any design catalogue.

To each his own… tagine

Manufactured in Flame® glazed clay, Emile Henry® tagines are particularly heat-resistant. They can be used in the oven, and can be placed directly on gas rings, electric plates and halogen hobs. Special attention is not required when using electric and halogen hobs, but it is strongly advised to increase the heat gradually. Only one important precaution must be taken: never place the empty tagine on a heat source.

With use, the glazed clay expands slightly creating the typical finely crackled effect in the enamel finish. It's the proof that the material reacts correctly to temperature change. It is a sign of resistance, and a long-life guarantee. The enamel finish is also scratch-resistant and very easy to clean. Emile Henry® tagines may be washed by hand or in the dishwasher, and, if necessary, may be left to soak to remove caramelised food.

When using the tagine for the first time, it is good practice to pour in enough milk to completely cover the bottom; bring the milk to the boil and then leave it to cool. Casein, the principal protein contained in milk has properties that are beneficial to glazed clay. After this simple initial operation, the tagine will be ready to cook any type of food, conserving full flavour.

If you are wondering which size is best for your needs, the Emile Henry line comes in three standard sizes: 25, 32 or 35 cm (9.8, 12.6, or 13.8 inch) diameters. Whether for a romantic dinner for two or for a table full of friends, there is a tagine for every occasion.

.

A few tips from the chef

For better results   In Western cuisine, meat and poultry are often browned first before they are left to braise. This is done in order to obtain a complex consistency: tender morsels wrapped in an outer layer that is crisper and darker in colour. Many of the recipes in this book use this technique to achieve a result that is closer to the taste that is more familiar to us. However, it is not necessary. In North Africa, home of the tagine, very often the same basic ingredients are placed in the base without browning, and are also subjected to longer cooking time for two main reasons: the use of cuts and types of meat which are different from those we are accustomed to, and the need to produce a dish that is extremely tender, suitable for being broken up and eaten with the hands. This teaches us that when cooking meat and poultry, the same tagine can produce both types of food. If you wish to obtain a dish with a more "European" flavour and appearance, after browning the main ingredient, add the other components at different times to control the consistency of the final dish, and to maintain the various ingredients distinct from one another. On the other hand, if you desire a dish which has a "stewed casserole" effect, all the components should be placed in the base together at the same time, and the cooking time extended. Do bear in mind that with fish and shellfish, cooking time must be kept to a minimum to retain flavour, aroma and consistency.

Maintaining correct humidity levels inside the tagine   This cooking utensil must never remain dry. Given the differences in raw ingredients it is not easy to give accurate estimates of the amount of liquid (water, broth, etc) to be added during the cooking process. Remember that the tagine is not hermetically sealed so it is inevitable that a certain amount of cooking vapour will evaporate. That is why it is important to check the ingredients regularly during cooking to insure they do not dry out too quickly.

The cooking process continues off heat   Flame® glazed clay utensils accumulate and maintain heat and transmit it back into the food even after the tagine has been removed from the direct heat source. This must be kept in mind, especially when preparing food such as fish and shellfish which cook very rapidly.

The tagine – from hob to table   The tagine is the perfect serving dish for convivial meals and can be taken directly from the hob and placed on the table. Do remember to take all due precautions to protect delicate surfaces from its accumulated heat. It is also advisable to warn guests that the tagine will remain very hot for several minutes.

Rice

Bulgur

Corn flour
(polenta)

Pasta

Not only couscous

A wide variety of cereals or
pasta can be cooked in a tagine:
traditional couscous, rice,
bulgur, pasta and polenta.

Couscous

Puréed peas with quadrucci pasta

For **4** servings
Preparation:
15 minutes
Cooking time:
20 minutes

500 g (1.1 lbs) of freshly shelled peas
120 g (4.2 oz) of fresh quadrucci pasta (short-cut pasta)
100 g (3.5 oz) of parmesan cheese
2 slices of raw-cured ham (prosciutto)
1 shallot
1 litre (4 cups) of vegetable broth
Extra virgin olive oil
Salt and pepper

Chop up the shallot and the ham (prosciutto).
Heat a drizzle of extra virgin olive oil in the tagine base and sauté the ham (prosciutto) with the shallot. Add 400 grams (14 oz) of peas, the broth, salt and pepper to taste and then cover with the lid and simmer for 15 minutes.

In another saucepan, parboil the rest of the peas (100 grams/ 3.5 oz) in salted water and drain. Shell the peas by making a small slit with the tip of a knife. Season with extra virgin olive oil, salt and pepper, and keep warm.

Using a small immersion mixer, blend the peas that have been cooked in the tagine in their broth. Add the quadrucci pasta, cover with the lid, and cook for just enough time for the pasta to cook (about 4-6 minutes).

When this dish is ready, add the whole peas which were kept aside and mix well with a dash of extra virgin olive oil and the grated parmesan cheese.

Serve piping hot.

Bulgur and aubergine tagine with herbs and hot mozzarella cheese

For **4** servings
Preparation:
10 minutes
Cooking time:
18 minutes

400g (14 oz) of bulgur
12 slices of sun-dried tomatoes
2 medium sized aubergines/eggplants
2 mozzarella cheeses, approx. 90 g (3 oz) each
3-4 cloves of garlic
1 pint (2 cups) of vegetable broth
Dried oregano
Dried thyme
Fresh basil
Extra virgin olive oil
Salt and pepper

Dice the aubergines/eggplants into small cubes and sauté lightly in the tagine with the crushed garlic cloves and the basil in a little extra virgin olive oil. Transfer to another container and set aside.

Heat a small amount of extra virgin olive oil in the tagine and add the bulgur. Toast for a few minutes, add the broth and cover with the lid. Cook on a medium heat for about 15 minutes stirring frequently, as for a risotto. Add more broth if necessary to make sure the bulgur does not become too dry.
Add the eggplants prepared previously.

Switch off the heat under the tagine. Add a dash of extra virgin olive oil and cook the bulgur and the aubergines/eggplants until creamy, add salt and pepper to taste. Garnish with the slices of dried tomato and arrange the slices of mozzarella over the tomato. Sprinkle with dried herbs. Cover with the lid and leave until the accumulated heat in the tagine melts the mozzarella.

Serve piping hot.

Vegetable soup with tortelli

For 4 servings
Preparation:
45 minutes
Resting time:
1 hour
Cooking time:
10 minutes

Radicchio tortelli
200 g (7 oz) all-purpose flour
2 eggs

1 head of red radicchio
1 small onion
50 g (1.76 oz) of coarsely
chopped smoked pork belly
(bacon or pancetta)
50 g (1.76 oz) of grated
Parmesan cheese
Extra virgin olive oil

Vegetable soup
4 cherry tomatoes
4 radishes
4 small eggs
4 small ceps or porcini
mushrooms
3 small zucchini or courgettes
1 stick of celery
1 large carrot
1 handful of spinach
Approx. 2 pints (4 cups)
of vegetable broth
Grated Parmesan cheese

Radicchio tortelli

Remove leaves from the radicchio head, wash and dry leaves.
Pour a dash of extra virgin olive oil into the tagine base and sauté the chopped onion, then add the pork belly (bacon or pancetta) and the radicchio. Cook for about 10 minutes on a low heat.
When cooked, chop all ingredients with a knife, add the grated Parmesan cheese and mix well. Keep the filling in the refrigerator until ready to use.

Make a well in the flour on the pastry board, mix in the eggs and knead thoroughly until the dough is silky smooth. Roll into a ball, wrap in kitchen film and leave it for 1 hour in a cool place.
Roll out the dough till very thin. Using a pasta cutter, cut out disks with a diameter of about 4-5 cm (1.5 to 2 inches) and fill with the radicchio filling. Fold over to form a crescent and seal edges well pressing them together with the prongs of a fork. .

Vegetable soup

Clean the mushrooms carefully eliminating all traces of soil.
Dice the larger vegetables into small pieces (the mushroom heads may be left whole if small).
Place all the vegetables in the tagine base which was used to cook the filling. Cover with the broth and simmer on low heat for about 10 minutes with the lid on (the vegetables should remain slightly crisp). When almost cooked, add the whole eggs, followed by the tortelli, and cook till ready.

Serve the vegetable soup in individual bowls with a drop of extra virgin olive oil and a sprinkling of Parmesan cheese.

Bean, pasta and shellfish tagine

Per **4** servings
Preparation:
12 hours to soak
the beans,
3-4 hours to purge
the shellfish
Cooking time:
40 minutes

500 g (1.1 lbs) of mixed
dried beans of choice in equal
portions (borlotti beans, black
beans, zolfini beans, cannellini
beans, Spello risina beans,
Spello cocco beans)
1 kg (2 lbs) of mixed shellfish
(carpet shell clams, baby
clams, mussels)
200 g (7 oz) of broken up
egg pasta
50 g (1.75 oz) of diced pork
belly (bacon or pancetta)
50 g (1.75 oz) of diced cooked
ham
2 Roma tomatoes
1 pint of vegetable broth
1 sprig of rosemary
1 bunch of parsley
1 clove of garlic
Thyme
Extra virgin olive oil

Soak all the beans in cold water for 12 hours, drain and place them in a large saucepan with slightly salted cold water and a sprig of rosemary. Bring to the boil and cook for about 30 minutes. The beans must still be left crisp because they will continue to cook when placed in the tagine.

Place the mussels and clams in separate containers and cover with cold salted water. Clean the mussels with a knife or hard brush to remove any residue, and pull out the beard. The clams need to soak for a longer time (3-4 hours) to purge the sand from the valves. It is best to change the water several times and to move the clams around using your hands, rubbing them lightly against one another.

Heat a little extra virgin olive oil in the base of the tagine and sauté the crushed garlic clove with the chopped parsley. Add the pork belly (bacon or pancetta), the ham, the chopped tomatoes and the beans drained from their cooking water. Add enough broth to cover the ingredients. Cover with the lid and continue cooking the beans for another 5 minutes.

Add the broken pasta pieces and all the shellfish and complete cooking, keeping the lid on. Only a few minutes are needed to open the shellfish and cook the pasta.
Sprinkle the dish with thyme leaves, a dash of raw extra virgin olive oil and serve at room temperature.

Stockfish tagine with fried polenta

For 4 servings

Preparation:

3 days to soak the
stockfish
3-4 hours to cook and
cool the polenta

Cooking time:

1 hour

1 stockfish* fillet
(approx. 1 kg/2 lbs)
3 cooking tomatoes
1 onion
5-6 celery leaves
1 untreated lemon
1 bunch of parsley
A few sprigs of thyme
Extra virgin olive oil
4-5 grains of black pepper
Salt and pepper

500 g (1.1 lbs) of stone-ground
corn flour (coarse grain)
Half a pint of water
Salt
Sunflower seed oil

* Unsalted cod-fish preserved
through exposure to sun and
wind at cold temperatures on
wooden racks in special drying
houses.

Leave the stockfish to soak in cold water for three days, changing the water several times.

Place the stockfish, a mixed bunch of celery leaves, 5-6 sprigs of parsley, the black pepper grains and the sliced lemon in a large saucepan. Add enough water to cover the ingredients, bring to the boil, and cook on medium heat for about 15 minutes. Drain off the cooking water, leave the stockfish to cool and then break it up into pieces.

During this time prepare a fairly consistent polenta. Once it has cooled, cut into lozenge-shaped pieces and put it aside.

Sauté the chopped onion with a dash of extra virgin olive oil in the tagine base. Add the stockfish and two ladles of tomato sauce obtained by blending raw tomatoes in a food processor without any further heating. Add salt and pepper to taste, add the thyme leaves, cover with the lid and cook on a low heat for about 45 minutes, checking to make sure it does not dry out.

When the stockfish is almost ready, fry the polenta pieces in a pan with plenty of sunflower seed oil. Drain them on kitchen paper to absorb all excess oil.

Serve the stockfish garnished with the fried polenta. For extra taste, this dish can be served with a green sauce made from chopped capers, anchovies, garlic, parsley and extra virgin olive oil.

Seafood tagine with herbs and spices

For **4** servings

Preparation:

3-4 hours to purge
the seafood
40 minutes for the rest
of the fish

Cooking time:

14 minutes

2 fillets of sole
2 mullets (mahi mahi or tilapia)
4 scallops
4 king prawns
4 scampi or langoustines
4 prawns
16 mussels
24 carpet shell clams
4-6 cherry tomatoes
1 small onion
Half a cup of vegetable broth
Celery leaves
A bunch of parsley
A pinch of saffron
A pinch of turmeric
Fresh oregano
Extra virgin olive oil
Salt and pepper

Fillet the soles and the mullet (mahi mahi or tilapia). Remove the scallop shells and separate the corals from the scallop meat. Remove the shells from the shellfish leaving the heads attached. Eliminate the intestinal tracts from the large prawns and the scampi or langoustines.

Place the mussels and clams in a separate container in cold salted water. Clean the mussel shells using a knife or a hard brush to remove all residue, and pull out the beard. The clams need to soak for a long time (3-4 hours) to purge the sand from the valves. It is best to change the water several times and to move the clams around using your hands, rubbing the clams lightly against one another.

Wash the cherry tomatoes, peel the onion and slice it. Wash and chop the parsley and celery leaves.

Pour a dash of extra virgin olive oil into the tagine base and add the tomatoes, onion, celery leaves, oregano, parsley, saffron, turmeric, and a little vegetable broth. Add salt and pepper to taste and cook on a low heat for 5-7 minutes.

Add the filleted fish, the seafood and shell fish in that order. Add salt and pepper to taste, and cover with the lid. Cook for a few more minutes and then add the scallop corals. Switch off the heat, but leaving the lid on the base. The steam vapour that is created inside the tagine will complete the cooking process. (about 5-6 minutes).

Serve as preferred, with aromatic wild rice as a side dish.

Salt cod tagine with olives

For **4** servings
Preparation:
10 minutes
Cooking time:
45 minutes

800 g (1.7 lbs) pre-soaked salt
cod
150 g (5.3 oz) of sun-dried
taggiasca olives (or Kalamata
olives)
2 potatoes
1 red onion
2 cloves of garlic
2 sprigs of rosemary
A bunch of parsley
1 spoonful of salt preserved
capers
½ lemon
½ untreated orange
Extra virgin olive oil

Heat the extra virgin olive oil in the tagine base with half the chopped parsley and the onion sliced in quarters. Sauté over a very low heat, and when the ingredients are soft, place the slices of cod on top.
Drizzle with a little extra virgin olive oil, cover with the lid and cook for about 30 minutes, taking care to add a little water flavoured with a few drops of lemon juice from time to time. When cooked, put the cod and onion mixture aside.

Peel the potatoes and slice finely. Brown them on a high heat in the tagine base with a dash of extra virgin olive oil, the rosemary and the cloves of garlic. When they are soft, add the cod, the onions, the dried olives, the finely sliced orange peel, the capers (rinsed to remove the salt), and a few sprigs of parsley. Replace the lid and leave for a few minutes for the ingredients to absorb the flavours.

This dish may be served with a citrus-flavoured mayonnaise.

King prawn tagine with capsicum/bell peppers and "green herb bread"

Per **4** servings
Preparation:
20 minutes
Cooking time:
15 minutes

16 king prawns
2 red capsicum/bell peppers
1 yellow capsicum/bell pepper
1 green capsicum/bell pepper
6 slices of sun-dried tomatoes
1 clove of garlic
Extra virgin olive oil
Salt and pepper

Green bread
3 slices of white bread
1 small garlic clove
1 small bunch of basil
1 small bunch of parsley

Remove the intestinal tract from the king prawns, make an incision on the back and leave the heads attached. Refrigerate until ready to use.

Wash the capsicum/bell peppers, dry well and remove all seeds and internal white filaments. Slice into fine strips.

Pour a dash of extra virgin olive oil into the tagine base, add the crushed garlic clove, the capsicum/bell peppers and the dried tomato slices. Add salt and pepper to taste and replace the lid. Cook for about 8-10 minutes on a medium heat.

Add salt and pepper to the king prawns, arrange them on top of the peppers and drizzle with a little extra virgin olive oil. Replace the lid and cook for 4-5 minutes.

Place the bread slices, aromatic herbs and the garlic clove into the bowl of a food processor or blender and process on high speed. The mixture should take on a bright green colour.

Sprinkle the serving dish with the green bread crumbs, then cover with the peppers and arrange the king prawns on top. Serve with a drizzle of extra virgin olive oil.

Fried shrimp tagine
with citrus vegetable chutney

For **4** servings
Preparation:
20 minutes
Marinating time:
4 hours
Cooking time:
15 minutes

16 large shrimp
1 onion
1 black garlic clove *
Corn flour (polenta)
Extra virgin olive oil
Salt and pepper

Chutney
8 firm cherry tomatoes
1 zucchini or courgette
1 red capsicum (bell) pepper
1 belgian endive
1 untreated lime
A piece of fresh ginger
A pinch of curry
Juice of 1 orange
1 cup of raspberry flavoured
vinegar (obtained by blending
white wine vinegar with
10 fresh raspberries).
Granulated sugar equal to the
weight of the vegetables.

Wash and trim the tomatoes, zucchini or courgette, endive and capsicum (bell) pepper.
Dice the vegetables (but leave the cherry tomatoes whole), placing them all in a bowl, then add the sugar, the raspberry vinegar, the orange juice, the diced lime (including the rind), the grated ginger, and the curry. Cover and leave to marinate for about 4 hours.

Transfer the vegetables and marinade to a saucepan and cook over medium heat until the cooking liquid assumes a syrupy consistency (about 10 minutes).

Clean the shrimp removing the heads, shells and intestinal tract. Add salt and pepper to taste, and toss them in the corn flour (polenta).
Pour a dash of extra virgin olive oil into the tagine base and cook the sliced onion and crushed (unpeeled) garlic clove. When they are transparent, add the shrimp, cover with the lid and simmer on low heat for about 5 minutes.

Place the citrus vegetable chutney into small bowls, arrange the shrimp on top and serve with sesame crackers.

*This is naturally fermented garlic from Asia. The natural fermentation process changes the pulp colour radically and has a strong influence on the final taste which is much sweeter with hints of soya and dried fruit.

Chicken tagine with wild chicory

For **4** servings
Preparation:
15 minutes
Marinating time:
1 hour
Cooking time:
1 hour and 15 minutes

1 chicken (about 1.5 kg/3.3 lbs)
cut into small pieces.
1 onion
2 cloves of garlic
1 glass (20 cl) of gin
1 glass (20 cl) of white wine
2 heads of wild chicory
1 lemon
4 spoonfuls of powdered
mixed spices in equal
proportions (sweet paprika,
chilli pepper, curry, black
pepper, cocoa)
Extra virgin olive oil
Salt and pepper

Place the chicken in a bowl, sprinkle with gin, add the peeled garlic cloves and leave to marinate for 1 hour in the refrigerator, turning the pieces over from time to time. Remove the chicken from the marinade, dry the pieces on kitchen paper and roll in the powdered spices so that they are well-coated with the spice mix.

Place the small diced onion in the cold tagine with a dash of extra virgin olive oil, arrange the chicken pieces on top and begin cooking at very low heat until completely browned, keeping the lid on. Add a splash of white wine and if the ingredients become a little dry, add a small amount of water. Add salt and pepper to taste and continue to cook till ready (about 1 hour and 15 minutes).

Cook the wild chicory in boiling salted water. Drain and rinse in ice and water to "fix" the bright green colour. Dress with an emulsion of extra virgin olive oil, lemon juice, and salt.

Serve the chicken with the chicory and accompany with flatbread (piadina or pita).

Guinea fowl tagine
with dates and dried apricots

For **4** servings
Preparation:
10 minutes
Marinating time:
2 hours
Cooking time:
1 hour and 15 minutes

1 guinea fowl
cut into small pieces
1 carrot
2 celery sticks
1 onion
12 dried dates
12 dried apricots
250 ml (1 cup)
of Lambrusco wine
(or sweet cider)
2 tablespoons of honey
Peppermint leaves
Extra virgin olive oil
Salt and pepper

Thinly slice the carrots, celery sticks and the onion, and pour an emulsion of extra virgin olive oil, salt and pepper on the vegetables. Arrange the pieces of guinea fowl in a bowl, and pour in the marinade making sure that all pieces are coated evenly. Cover with kitchen film and leave to marinate in the refrigerator for 2 hours.

Heat some extra virgin olive oil in the tagine and add the guinea fowl (after having removed it from the marinade), brown all the pieces well, then cover with the lid and cook on low heat. After about an hour, add the dates and the dried apricots, splash with some Lambrusco (or cider) and drizzle the honey on top. When the dish is almost cooked, add the mint leaves. The guinea fowl is ready when the flesh can be easily removed from the drumstick bone.

This dish may be served with an oriental long grained rice (Thai or Basmati).

Chicken tagine
with caramelised citrus fruit

For **4** servings
Preparation:
20 minutes
Marinating time:
1 hour
Cooking time:
45 minutes

12 chicken legs (drumsticks)
150 g (5.3 oz) of brown sugar
2 oranges
2 lemons
1 grapefruit
1 lime
1 red onion
The juice of half a pineapple
1 garlic clove
Rosemary
Extra virgin olive oil
White wine
Balsamic vinegar
Salt and pepper

Trim the chicken legs, and place them in a dish with the salt, pepper, rosemary, crushed garlic, chopped onion, white wine and a drizzle of extra virgin olive oil. Leave to marinate for about an hour then transfer all the ingredients to the tagine base. Cover and cook over low heat for approximately 40 minutes.

In the meantime peel all the citrus fruit and separate each segment from the membrane. (If the fruit is untreated, it can be cut into segments without removing the peel). Sprinkle with brown sugar and add the citrus fruit to the chicken legs after about ¾ of the cooking time. When the dish is cooked, add the pineapple juice, mix well and reduce the cooking glaze to a syrup consistency. The chicken legs should have a pleasant glazed finish.

Serve the chicken legs with the caramelised fruit and a few drops of balsamic vinegar.

Duck tagine with lemon balm flavoured figs

For **4** servings
Preparation:
5 minutes
Cooking time:
12 minutes

4 duck breasts
12 black figs
1 onion
250 ml (1 cup) of Lambrusco
wine (or sweet cider)
1 clove of garlic
1 sprig of rosemary
1 bunch of lemon balm
2 tablespoons of brown sugar
Balsamic vinegar
Extra virgin olive oil
Salt and pepper

Place the chopped onion in the tagine with a little extra virgin olive oil. Arrange the figs over the onions and sprinkle the ingredients with the brown sugar and lemon balm leaves. Pour over the Lambrusco (or cider), cover with the lid, and cook on high heat until the figs are caramelised and the cooking glaze has a syrupy consistency (about 6-8 minutes).

Separately, cut the duck breasts with the skin into large cubes. Pour a little extra virgin olive oil into a pan, add the garlic clove and rosemary. Add the pieces of duck and brown on high heat for a couple of minutes. This will help eliminate a large part of the duck fat. When the meat is well-browned, add salt and pepper and transfer the duck to the tagine base to blend the flavours and complete the cooking process. (about 3-4 minutes).

To serve, arrange the duck on a bed of figs and lemon balm, garnish with a few drops of balsamic vinegar and serve with flaky pastry puffs and squaquerone cheese.

.

Quail tagine with fruit and vegetables

For **4** servings
Preparation:
20 minutes
Cooking time:
20 minutes

8 quails
1 carrot
1 zucchini or courgette
1 eggplant
1 onion
4 cherry tomatoes
4 small fresh apricots
4 fresh plums
1 nectarine (unripe)
1 yellow peach (ripe)
Sage
Rosemary
Extra virgin olive oil
Salt and pepper

Clean the quails and cut them in half. Remove any excess fat especially around the neck cavity. Brown the quails in some extra virgin olive oil in the tagine base on high heat adding a few sprigs of sage and rosemary. Add salt and pepper, cover with the lid, and cook for 15 minutes. When the quails are cooked, transfer them to a dish, cover them and keep them warm.

Chop all the vegetables in large-sized pieces and sauté in extra virgin olive oil in a pan on high heat.

Remove the stones from the fruit, cut the apricots and plums in half, and the peaches and nectarines in quarters.
Take the tagine base in which the quails were cooked, add the pieces of fruit and a little extra virgin olive oil, and cook on high heat for a couple of minutes. Add the previously, cooked vegetables, arrange the quails on top, cover with the lid and switch off the heat. Leave the dish to absorb flavour for about 5-6 minutes.

To serve, arrange the quails on top of the fruit and vegetables in individual dishes, and serve with a dark beer flavoured with a few drops of lime juice.

Chicken wings in raspberry, garlic and mint vinegar sauce

For **4** servings
Preparation:
15 minutes
Cooking time:
40 minutes

24 chicken wings
3 potatoes
1 large aubergine/eggplant
100 g (3.5 oz) of fresh
raspberries
50 ml (approx. 1/4 cup)
of white vinegar
3 cloves of garlic
1 sprig of thyme
1 sprig of rosemary
Mint leaves
Vegetable broth
Extra virgin olive oil
Salt and pepper

Trim the chicken wings. Heat a little extra virgin olive oil in the tagine base, and add the two crushed garlic cloves, rosemary, and chicken wings. Begin cooking over low heat, raising the flame near the end to obtain a little colour. The chicken is cooked when the meat can be easily separated from the bone (approx. 30 minutes). Leave to cool and set aside.

Purée half the raspberries in a blender with the white vinegar and filter retaining the liquid.

Cut the mint into fine strips, chop one clove of garlic finely and add both to the raspberry and vinegar mixture. Add some extra virgin olive oil, whip to create an emulsion and serve cold on the chicken wings.

Cut the potatoes into fairly large pieces and brown them in a little extra virgin olive oil in the tagine base used for the chicken wings. Add a little vegetable broth, salt and pepper to taste, cover with the lid, and cook till ready. The potatoes should be soft but must not disintegrate (about 10 minutes).

Separately cut the eggplant into fairly large pieces, cook them in the oven at 170 °C (350 °F) with a little extra virgin olive oil and the thyme (15 minutes). When cooked, add the eggplant to the potatoes in the tagine. Leave to cool till tepid and add the cooled chicken wings. Garnish with the remaining fresh raspberries and serve.

Lamb tagine with potatoes and breadcrumb farofa

For **4** servings
Preparation:
15 minutes
Cooking time:
30 minutes

600 g (1.3 lbs) of leg of lamb, in pieces
4 large red potatoes
1 large onion
1 sprig of rosemary
2 bay leaves
1 teaspoon of coriander
Extra virgin olive oil
Salt and pepper

Breadcrumb Farofa*
200 g (7 oz) of breadcrumbs
1 clove of garlic
Dried thyme
Dried oregano
Fennel seeds
Extra virgin olive oil
Salt and pepper

* **Farofa**: this is a Brazilian dish whose main ingredient is manioca flour. This dish has the same consistency as polenta. In this recipe, the manioca flour has been replaced with breadcrumbs.

Peel the potatoes and cut them into large pieces. Toss them in extra virgin olive oil in the tagine base with the sprig of rosemary. When the potatoes are browned (about 10 minutes), add salt and pepper to taste and set aside.

Chop up the onion and place in the tagine adding a drizzle of extra virgin olive oil. When the onion is soft and transparent, add the meat, salt and pepper to taste and then the coriander and bay leaves. Cover with the lid and cook at low heat for about 20-30 minutes (it may be necessary to add a little broth or water to make sure the meat does not become too dry). When the meat is nicely tender, add the potatoes, mix them in to absorb flavour and continue to simmer for a few minutes. Remember that even when the heat is switched off the cooking process will continue because the tagine maintains its heat for quite a long time.

Breadcrumb Farofa
Toast the breadcrumbs in a pan in a little extra virgin olive oil, with the garlic clove, thyme, oregano, fennel seeds, and the salt and pepper. The farofa is ready when the breadcrumbs have toasted to a good colour. Sprinkle the lamb with the breadcrumb farofa just before serving.

Veal tagine with onions in dark beer

For **4** servings
Preparation:
15 minutes
Cooking time:
10-12 minutes

500 g (1.1 lbs) of thinly sliced
veal loin
330 ml (approx 1 1/3 cups) of
dark beer (such as Guinness)
1 slice of Italian raw-cured
ham (prosciutto) for each veal
slice
3 red onions
1 sage leaf for each veal slice
Sweet paprika to taste
Extra virgin olive oil
A knob of butter
Salt and pepper

Pound the veal slices between sheets of clingfilm until very thin. If necessary trim them to obtain slices of similar size. Place a slice of raw-cured ham (prosciutto) and a sage leaf on each veal slice, and attach together with a toothpick.
Place the veal slices in the tagine base with a little extra virgin olive oil and brown on both sides on high heat for about 3-4 minutes. Add salt and pepper to taste and set aside.

Slice the onions finely; place them in the unheated tagine base with a knob of butter and the beer. Cook on low heat for 6-8 minutes making sure they remain crisp.

Arrange the veal slices on the onions, sprinkle with a pinch of paprika, cover with the lid and simmer for a few more minutes.

To serve, arrange the veal slices in layers. Accompany with the onions and grilled polenta if desired.

Pork meatballs with zucchini and mint

For 4 servings
Preparation:
15 minutes
Cooking time:
18 minutes

Couscous
200 g (7 oz) of instant couscous
1 knob of butter
Extra virgin olive oil
1 small bunch of chives
Salt

Pork meatballs
400 g (14.1 oz) of finely minced pork
200 g (7 oz) of almond slivers

150 g (5.3 oz) of breadcrumbs
4 zucchini or courgettes
1 egg
2 cloves of garlic
6 mint leaves
1 sprig of rosemary
Extra virgin olive oil
Salt and pepper

Couscous
Place 250 ml (1 cup) of water, a generous drizzle of extra virgin olive oil and a pinch of salt in a large saucepan. Bring to boiling point, remove the saucepan from the heat, add the couscous and stir gently. Cover and leave the couscous grains to absorb the liquid for a few minutes in order to swell. Add a knob of butter, replace on the heat and continue to cook for another 3-4 minutes (stir the couscous continually with a fork to prevent lumps from forming) Add a sprinkling of chives immediately before serving.

Pork meatballs
Place the minced pork, the egg, the chopped garlic clove and chopped rosemary in a bowl and mix together well. Roll small amounts of the mixture between the palms of your hands to form meatballs and press them lightly to give them a slightly flattened shape.
Mix the breadcrumbs with the almonds and roll the meatballs in the mixture coating them well on all sides.
Brown the meatballs in extra virgin olive oil in the tagine base till they are cooked and add salt and pepper to taste. Remove the meatballs and set aside.

Cut the zucchini or courgettes into large pieces and season with the chopped garlic and the mint leaves. Place in the tagine base having removed the meatballs, and cook for 5-6 minutes. Now add the pork meatballs, and a little extra virgin olive oil. Cover with the lid and cook for another 4-5 minutes.

Serve the meatballs and vegetables in the tagine platter, accompanying them with the prepared couscous.

Lamb tagine in sweet and sour sauce with mixed nuts

For **4** servings
Preparation:
10 minutes
Cooking time:
14 minutes

16 lamb chops
200 g (7 oz) of diced fresh
pork belly (bacon or pancetta)
150 g (5.3 oz) of mixed nuts
(peanuts, walnuts, almonds
and salted pistachio nuts)
100 g (3.5 oz) of dried coconut
pulp (dessicated coconut)
12 dried apricots
8 dried dates
3 tablespoons of citrus honey
2 cloves of garlic
1 glass (20 cl) of green tea
The juice of 1 lemon
1 strongly perfumed
biologically grown rose
Extra virgin olive oil
Salt and pepper

Sauté the pork belly (bacon or pancetta) and the unpeeled garlic in a little extra virgin olive oil in the tagine base. Add the lamb chops and brown them for about 5-6 minutes on high heat. When they are almost done, add the apricots, dates and the green tea. Cover with the lid and continue to cook for a few minutes.

Add the mixed nuts, salt and pepper to taste, and after a few minutes, drizzle with the honey and lemon juice. Cover with the lid, switch off the heat and leave for 7-8 minutes.

Just before serving, sprinkle with dried coconut (keeping a little to decorate the serving dish) and the rose petals. Cover with the lid once more to let the coconut and rose petals melt slightly.

Serve the tagine, drizzling the meat with the cooking glaze and dried coconut. It may be served with beer flavoured with ginger and star anise.

Sausage and mushroom tagine with melted cheese

Per 4 servings
Preparazione:
25 minuti
Cottura:
12-15 minuti

8 sausages (Luganega type)
150 g (approx 5½ oz) semifirm cow's milk cheese such as toma, gruyère or Monterey Jack)
600 g (1.3 lbs) of mixed mushrooms (porcini or ceps, chiodini or honey mushrooms, chanterelles)
200 g (7 oz) of smoked pork belly (bacon or pancetta)
1 cup of broth

1 bunch of parsley
1 sprig of rosemary
1 garlic clove
4-5 sage leaves
Extra virgin olive oil
Coarse smoked salt

Clean the mushrooms carefully removing all traces of soil.
Dice the pork belly (bacon or pancetta) and finely chop the herbs.
Cut the sausage into small even pieces and pierce the skin with the prongs of a fork.

Lightly sauté the garlic clove and pork belly (bacon or pancetta) in a little extra virgin olive oil in the tagine base on low heat. When the pork belly takes on a little colour, add the mushrooms, raise the heat, and continue cooking.

Add the chopped herbs, and lower the heat after 5 minutes. Add the broth, then the sausage, cover with the lid and cook for a further 5-7 minutes.

Remove the tagine lid, arrange the wedges of cheese on the meat and mushrooms, then add a pinch of smoked salt, and replace the lid. Raise the heat again and cook just enough to melt the cheese (2-3 minutes).

This dish may be served with bruschetta (toasted slices of Italian bread rubbed with garlic and topped with tomato pulp).

Beef tagine with chicory and tomato

For **4** servings
Preparation:
10 minutes
Cooking time:
50 minutes

800 g (1.7 lbs) of beef sirloin
cut into large pieces
3 bunches of chicory
(or 1 large head of escarole
or curly endive)
3-4 cloves of garlic
4 tablespoons of double
tomato concentrate
1 chilli pepper
Extra virgin olive oil
Salt and pepper

Wash the chicory leaves and cut into small pieces.
Place the chopped garlic, chilli pepper, tomato concentrate, extra virgin olive oil, salt and pepper in the tagine base. Add a glass of water, cover with the lid and simmer on low heat for about 45 minutes, adding additional water from time to time if the ingredients start to dry out.

Separately in a pan, brown the beef with a little extra virgin olive oil and, when the meat is well-browned on all sides, transfer it to the tagine, placing it on the bed of chicory. Continue to cook for about 5-6 minutes. The dish is be ready when the cooking juices have reduced. Take great care not to let it reduce too far and become dry.

Rabbit meatballs
in lemon and rosemary cream

For **4** servings
Preparation
25 minutes
Cooking time:
10 minutes

600 g (1.3 lbs) rabbit meat
(from the leg)
400 ml (approx 1¾ cups)
of liquid cream
200 g (7 oz) of breadcrumbs
150 g (5.3 oz) of salted
pistachio nuts
1 slice of bread soaked
in a little milk
3 basil leaves
2 cloves of garlic
1 untreated lime
1 egg
1 sprig of rosemary
Nutmeg
Curry
Extra virgin olive oil
Salt and pepper

Place the cream, the rind of the lime sliced into very fine strips, torn basil leaves, and crushed garlic into the tagine and mix together. Reduce on a low heat for a few minutes; add salt and pepper to taste. This should have the aspect of a creamy sauce.

Pass the rabbit meat through the meat grinder twice on its finest setting. Add the bread (previously soaked in the milk, pressed and broken pieces) followed by the egg and a pinch of curry. Mix all the ingredients together well and roll to form round meatballs. Roll them in the breadcrumbs and brown them in a pan with extra virgin olive oil and the rosemary. Add salt and pepper to taste.

Transfer the meatballs into the tagine base with the sauce, and then sprinkle with the pistachio nuts and some grated nutmeg; mix well and serve very hot.

Pork and tomato tagine with sautéed rice

For **4** servings
Preparation:
25 minutes
Cooking time:
35 minutes

Sautéed rice
200 g (7 oz) risotto rice
such as Carnaroli or Arborio
150 g (5.3 oz) of grated
Parmesan cheese
1 shallot
1 glass of dry white wine
½ litre (2 cups) of meat broth
1 knob of butter
Extra virgin olive oil

Pork tagine
4 pork chops
4 small sausages
150 g (5.3 oz) of fresh pork
belly (pancetta)
4 cherry tomatoes
2 tablespoons of tomato
concentrate
½ litre (2 cups) of meat broth
1 small onion
1 stick of celery
1 small carrot
2 cloves of garlic
A pinch of saffron threads
Extra virgin olive oil
Salt and pepper

Sautéed rice
Melt the butter in a saucepan, add the chopped shallot, and when it is transparent, add the rice. Sauté the rice briefly, then add the wine. Let the wine evaporate and then add the hot broth a little at a time. Continue to cook the risotto (about 18 minutes) adding small amounts of broth gradually as it is absorbed by the rice. Remove from the heat, and mix well with the Parmesan cheese and a drop of extra virgin olive oil.
Leave the risotto to cool, then heat a little oil in a non-stick pan. Place the rice in the pan and press it firmly so that it forms a flat disk. Brown well on both sides and keep it warm.

Pork tagine
Cut the carrot, onion and celery into small pieces. Sauté the vegetables and the garlic lightly in a little extra virgin olive oil in the tagine base and cover with the lid for a short time. When the vegetables have softed and have taken on a pleasant aroma, add the chops, the sliced sausage (pierce the casing with the prongs of a fork) the pork belly, the cherry tomatoes, the tomato concentrate, the saffron threads and the broth.
Cover with the lid and cook on at very low heat for about 30 minutes. Check from time to time to insure that the cooking juices in the bottom of the pan have not evaporated, and add a little broth if necessary. Salt and pepper to taste. When the meat is tender enough to come away from the chop bone, the dish is ready.

Serve the pork tagine with a wedge of the sautéed rice cake.

Dried fruit tagine with a honey glaze

For **4** servings
Preparation:
15 minutes
Maceration:
48 hours
Cooking time:
6-7 minutes

8 dried apricots
4 stoned prunes
4 dates
4 fresh figs
4 slices of dried pineapple
1 unpeeled pear (Williams)
cut in quarters
1 unpeeled yellow peach
cut in pieces
4 fresh red plums
1 handful of sultana raisins
3 tablespoons of millefiori
honey
200 g (7 oz) of mixed nuts
(walnuts, hazel nuts, pistachio
nuts, pine nuts and almonds)
100 g (3.5 oz) of granulated
sugar
200 g (7 oz) of water
A pinch of citric acid (available
at chemists' shops)
Edible flowers (rose, jasmine,
elder flower petals)

Place the water and sugar in a heavy-bottomed saucepan and bring to a boil. Remove from heat, allow the syrup to cool and add most of the flower petals (reserving a few of each type for decoration).
Leave to macerate for 48 hours, filter the syrup and add a pinch of citric acid (this will prevent the formation of mould that can occur when vegetal matter is subjected to a lengthy period of infusion).

Place all of the fruit in the tagine base and pour in the syrup and honey. Cover with the lid and cook at very low heat for about 6-7 minutes. The fruit should be soft with a glazed surface.

Decorate with the remaining flower petals just before serving. This dish may be served with Bourbon vanilla ice-cream.

Index